Coloring book for adults and kids amazing rose image for design

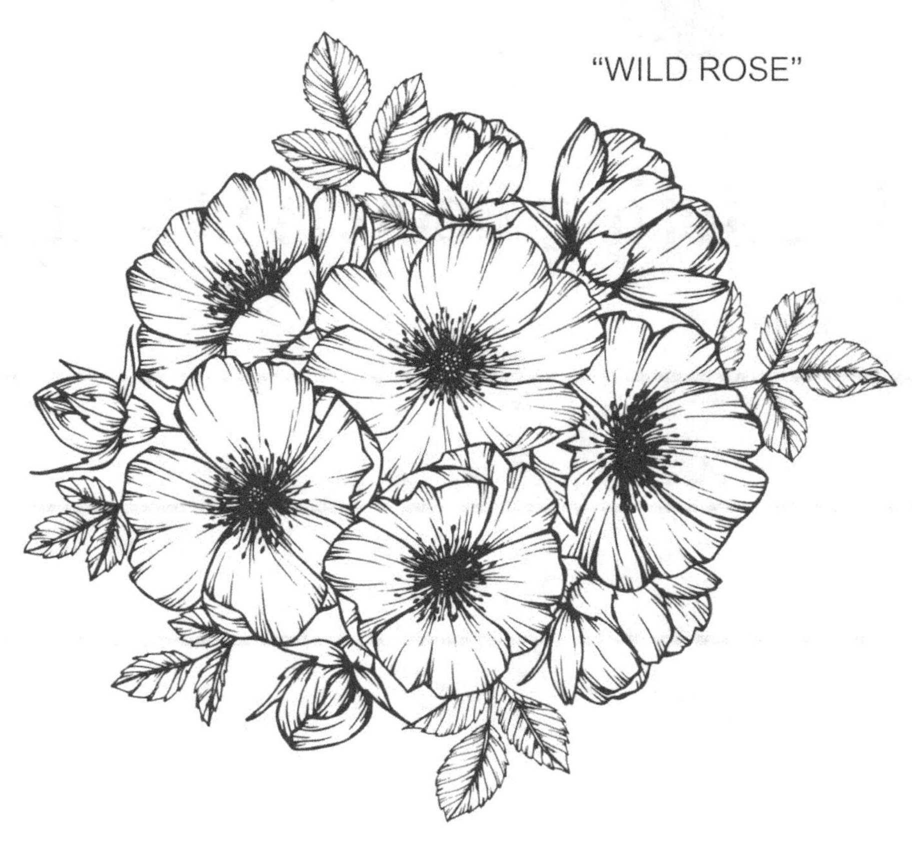

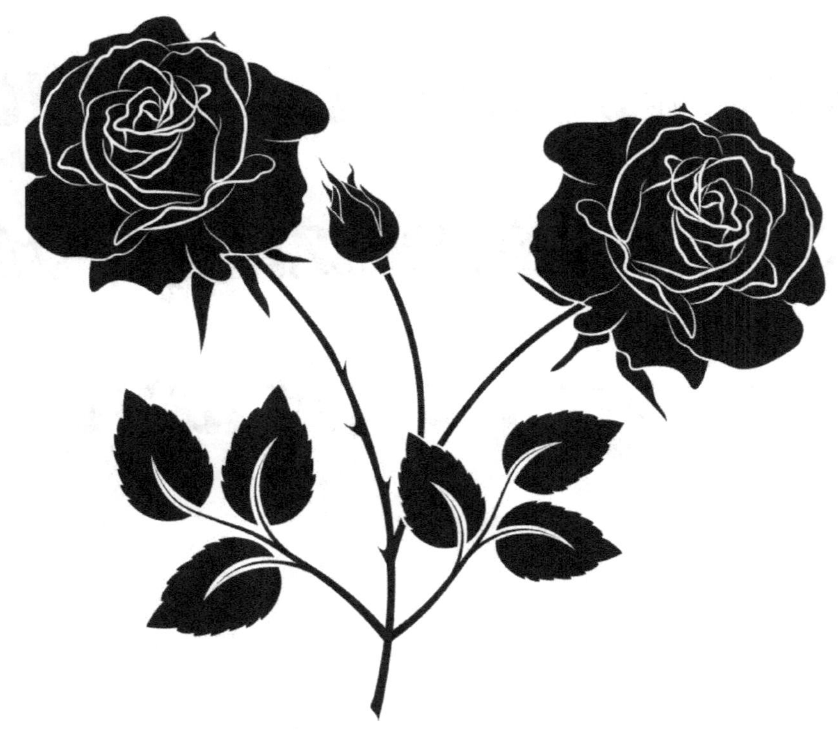

This coloring book is belongs to

____

____

____

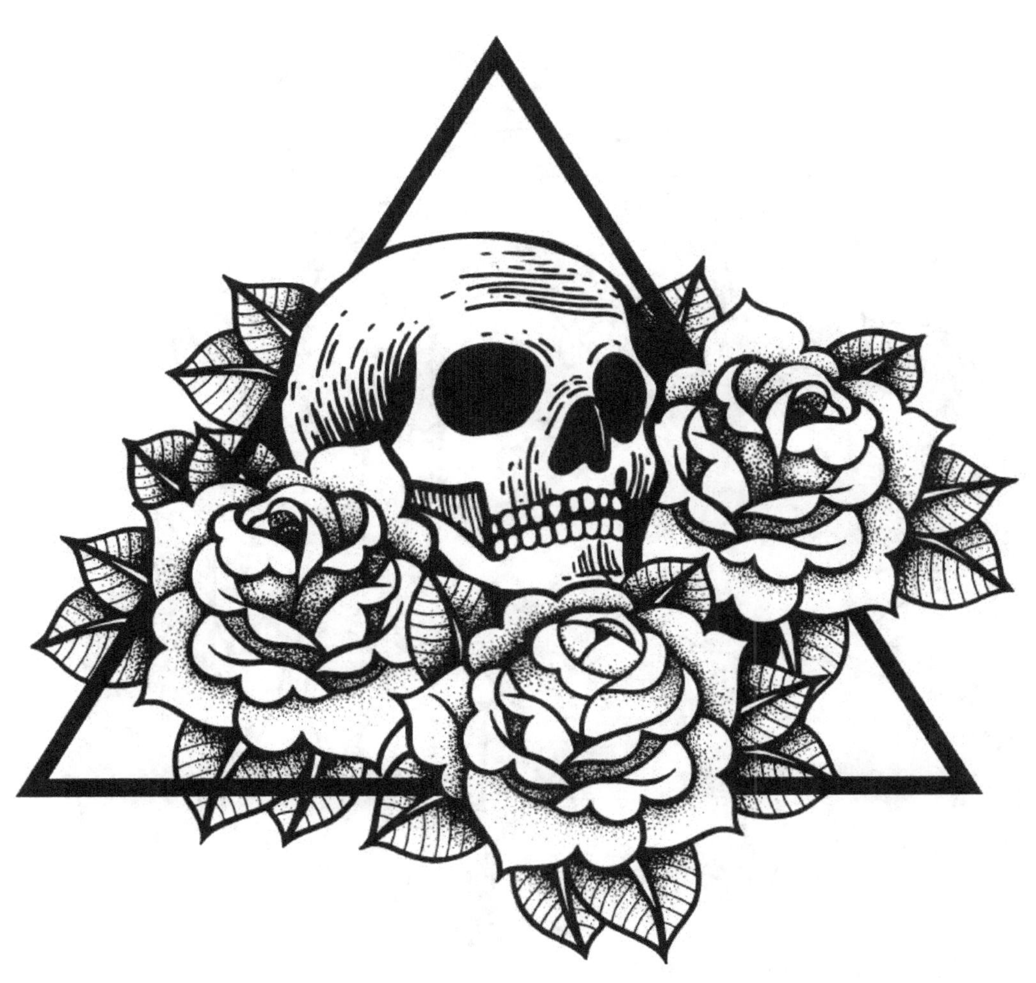

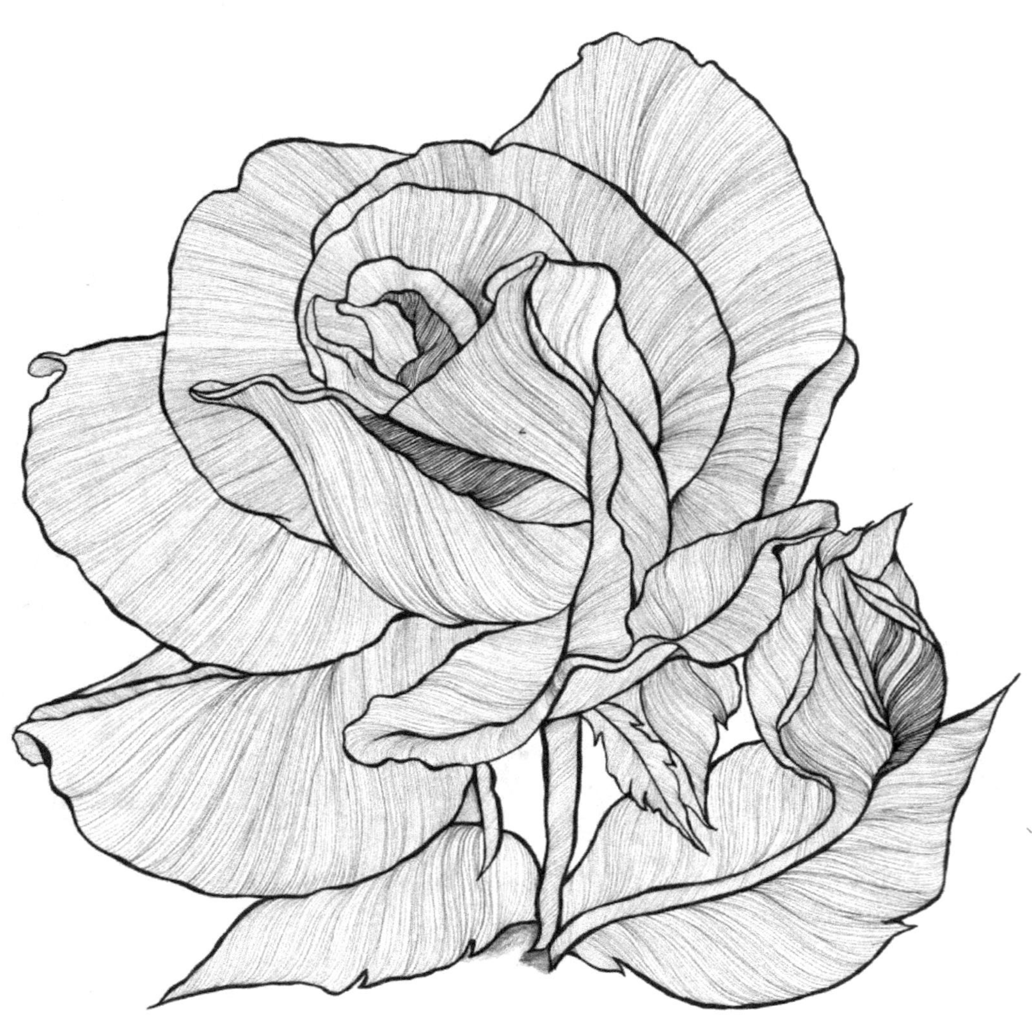

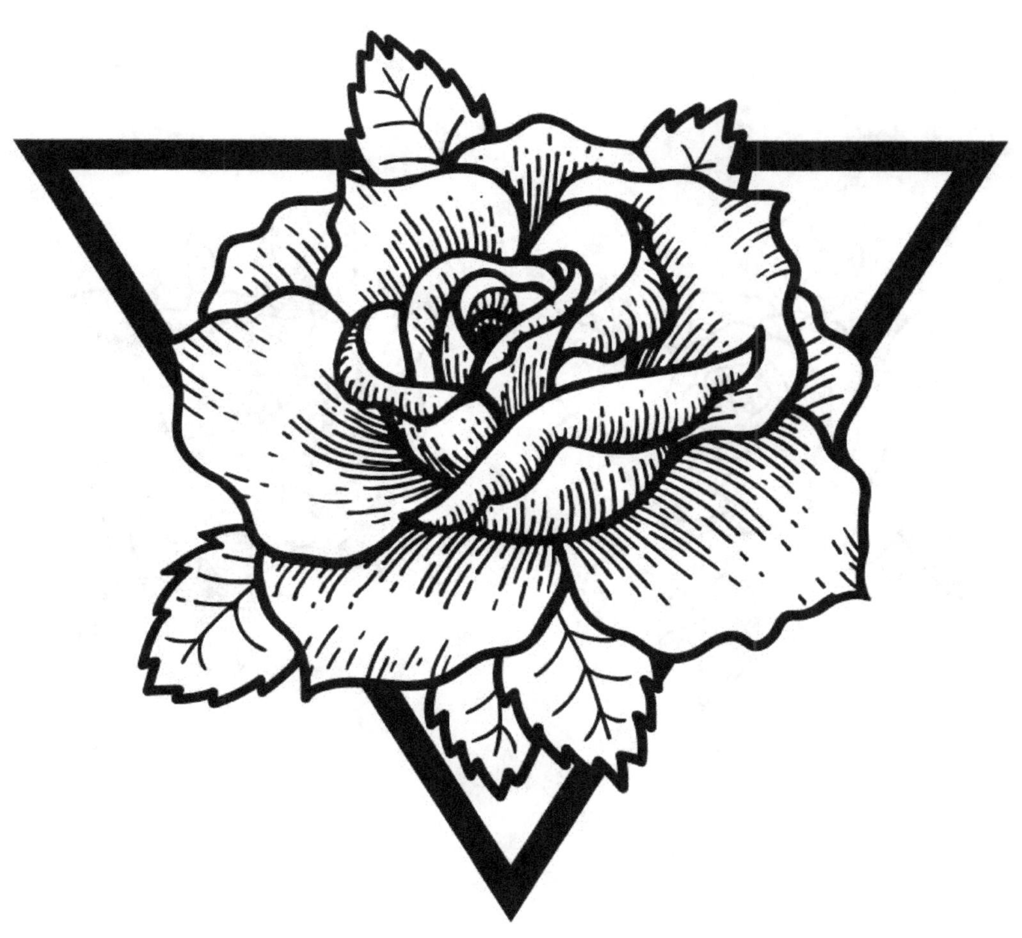

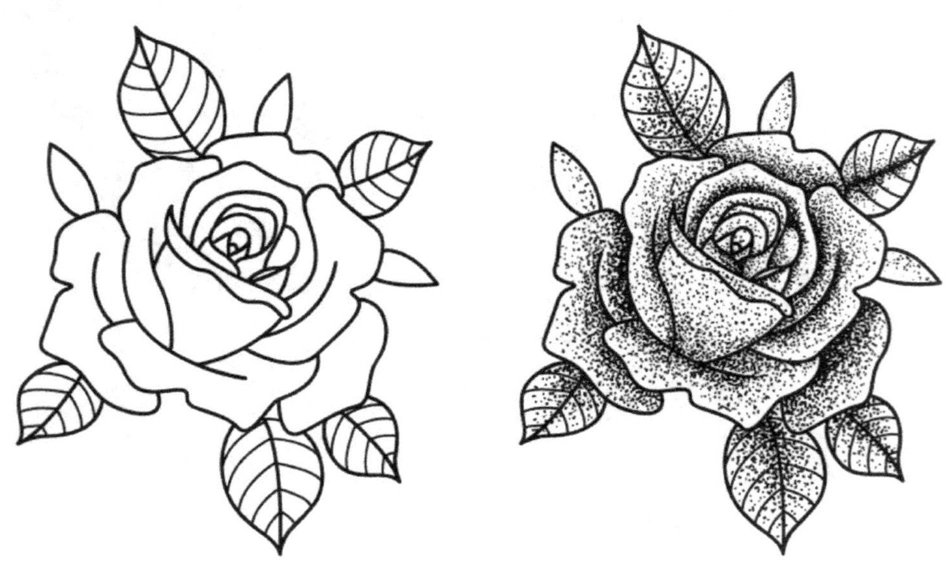

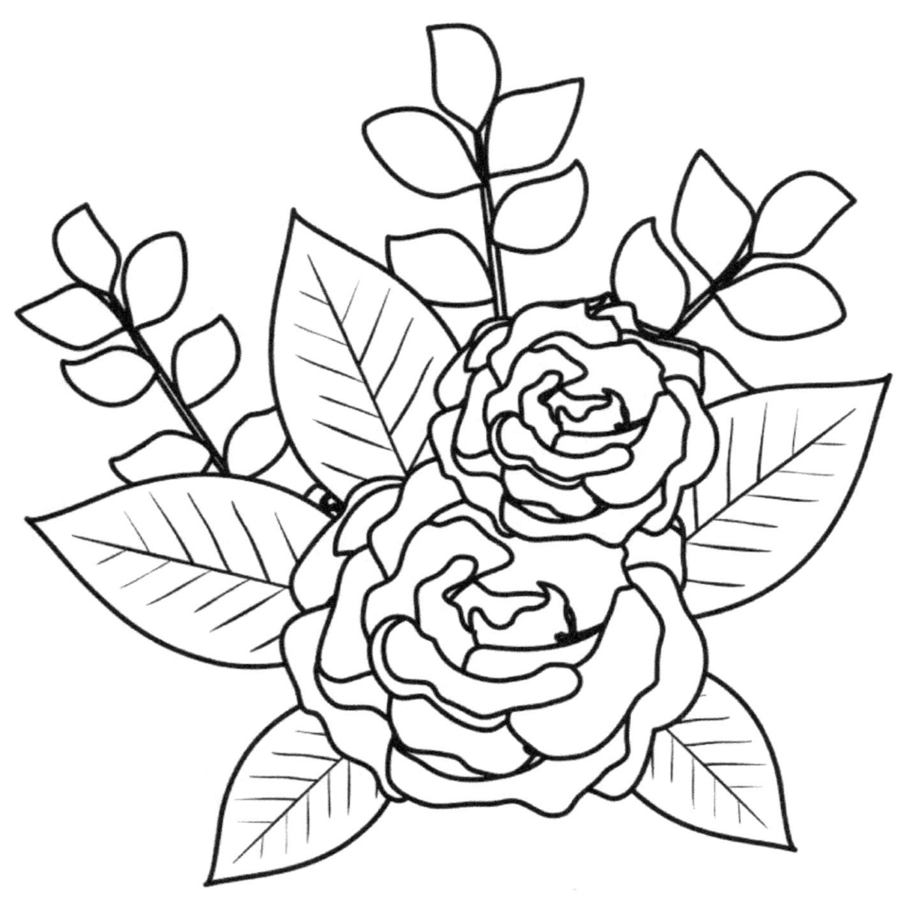

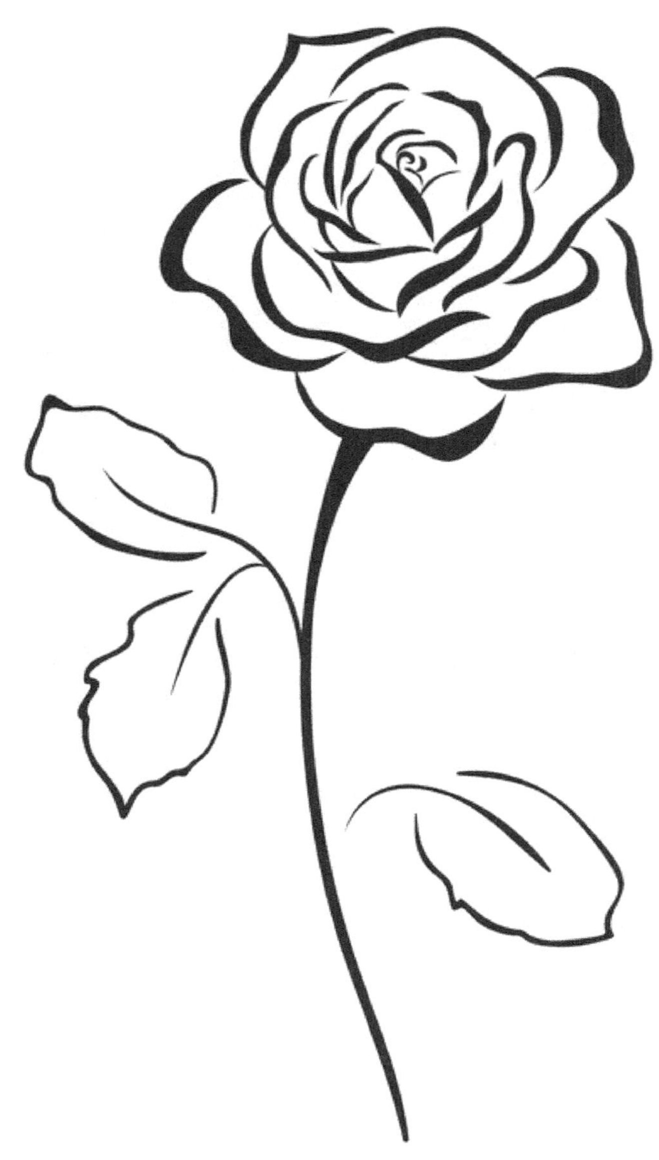

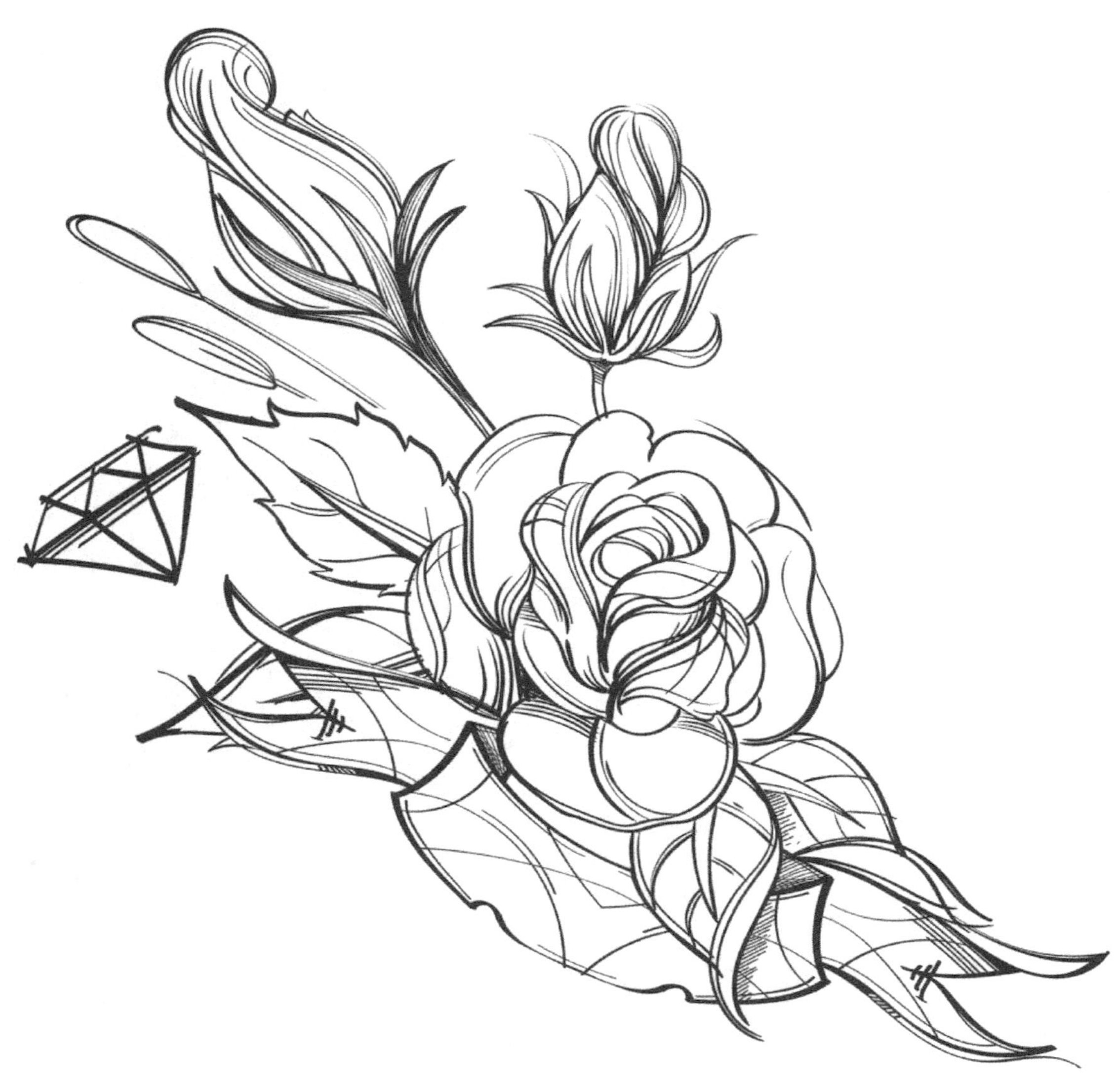

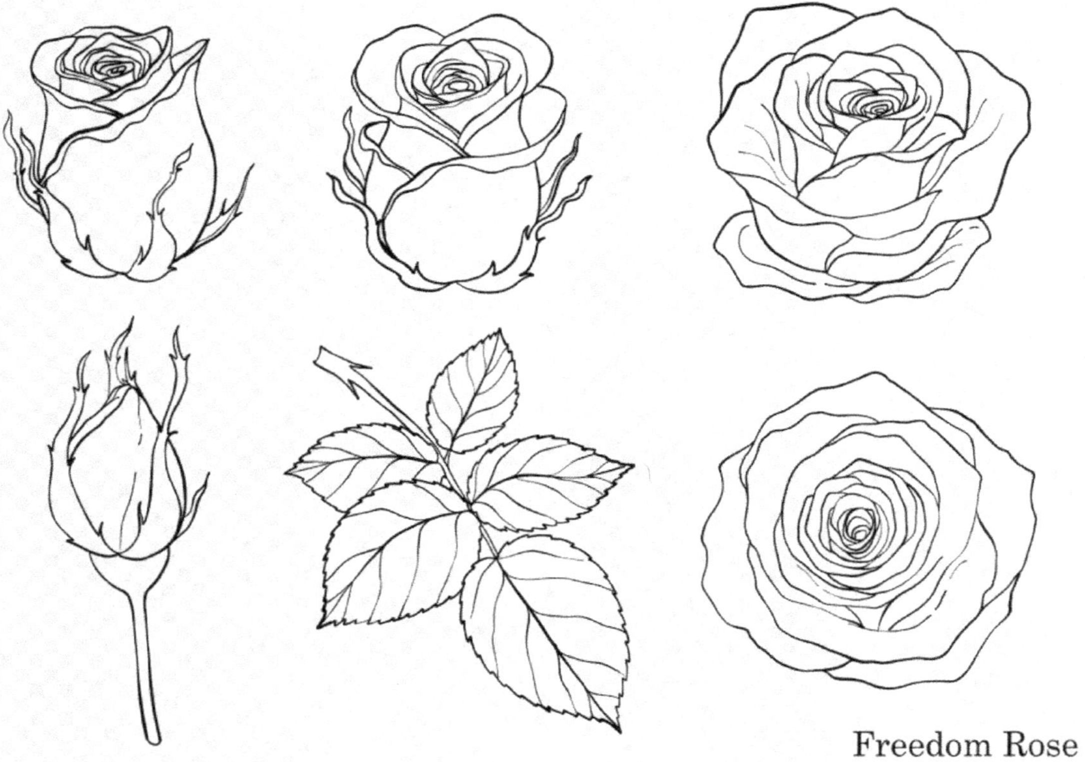

Freedom Rose

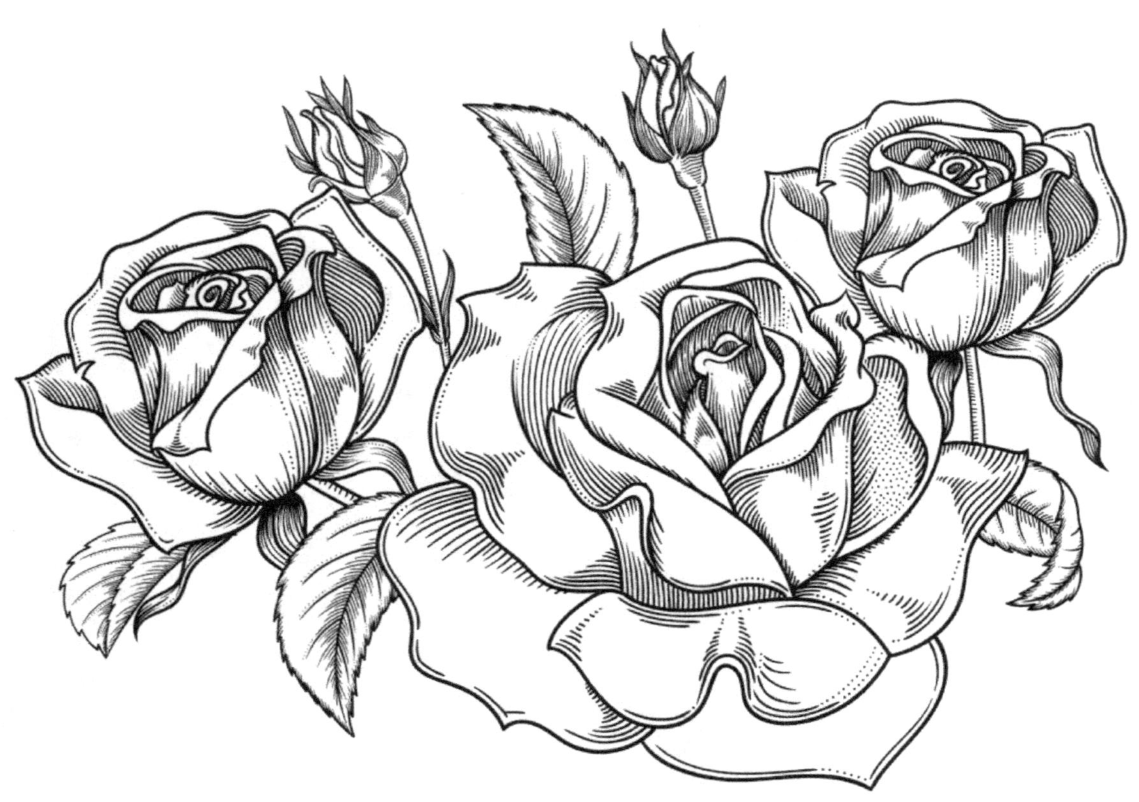

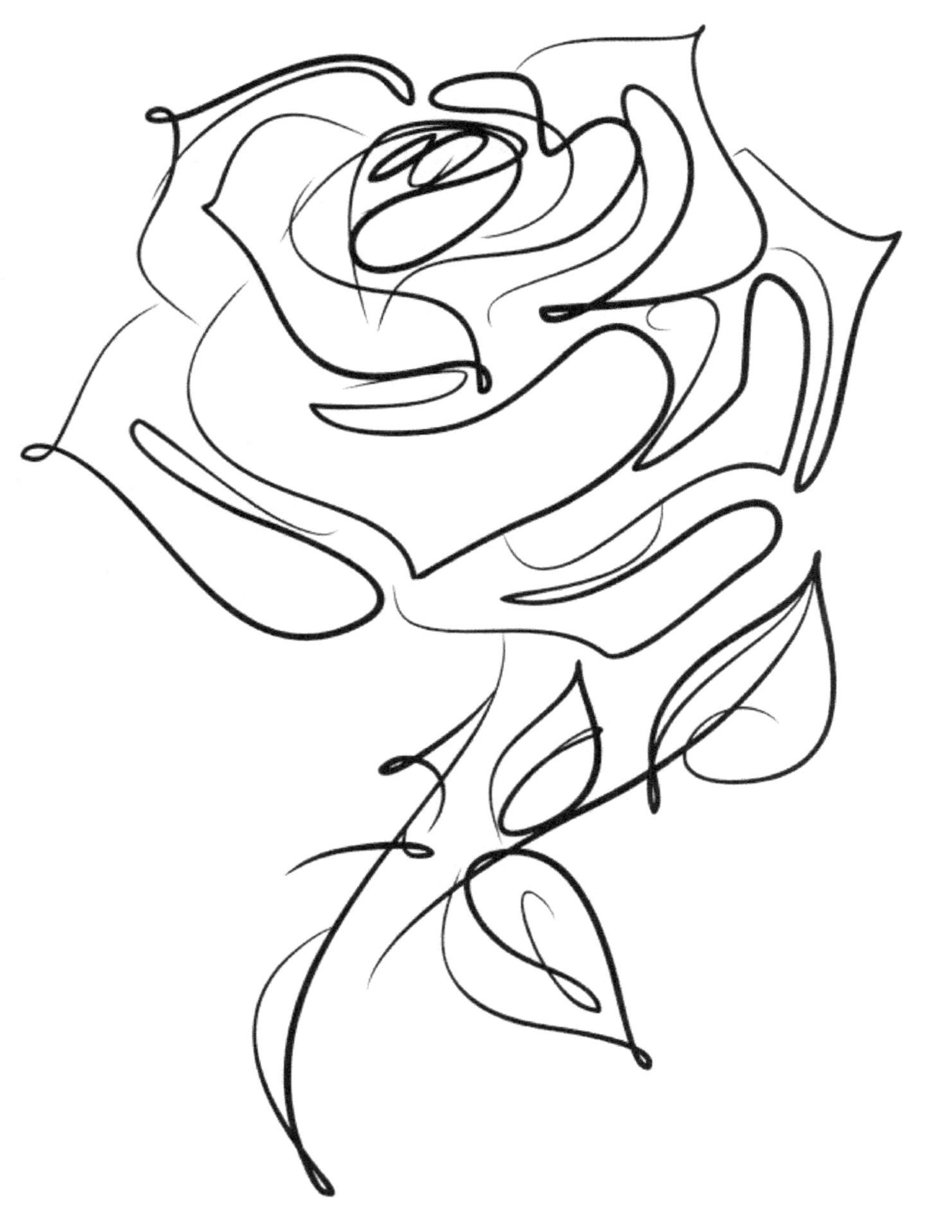

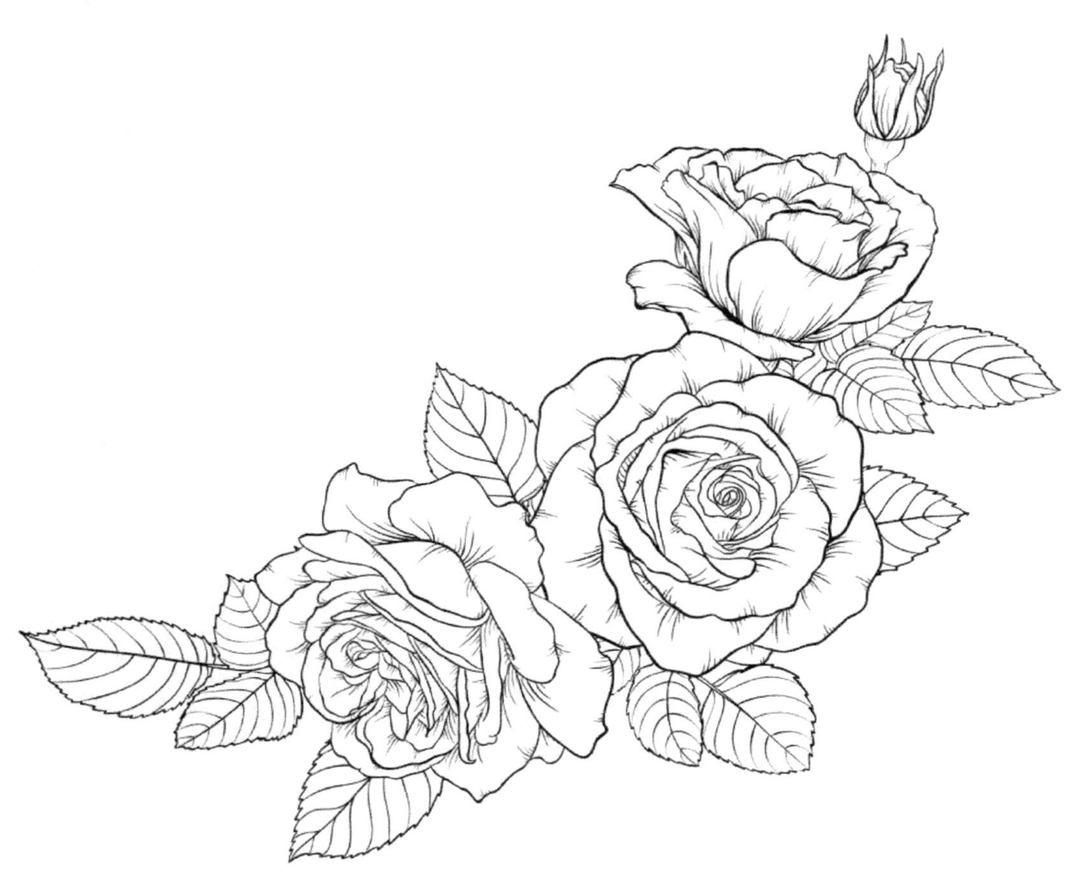

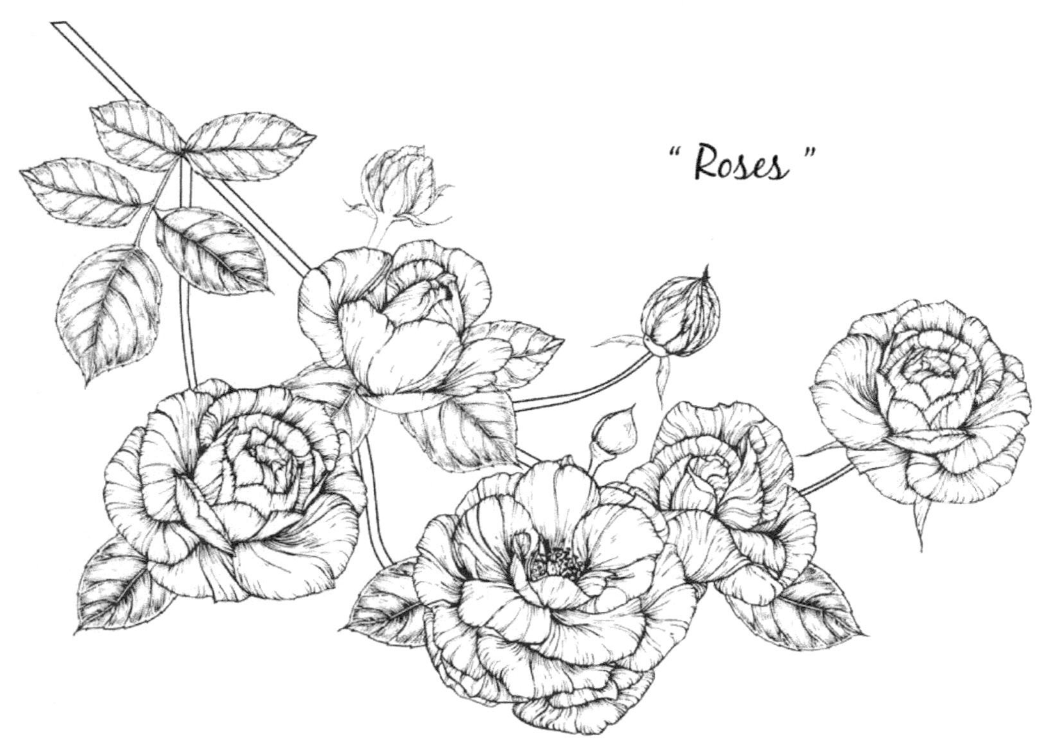

" Roses "

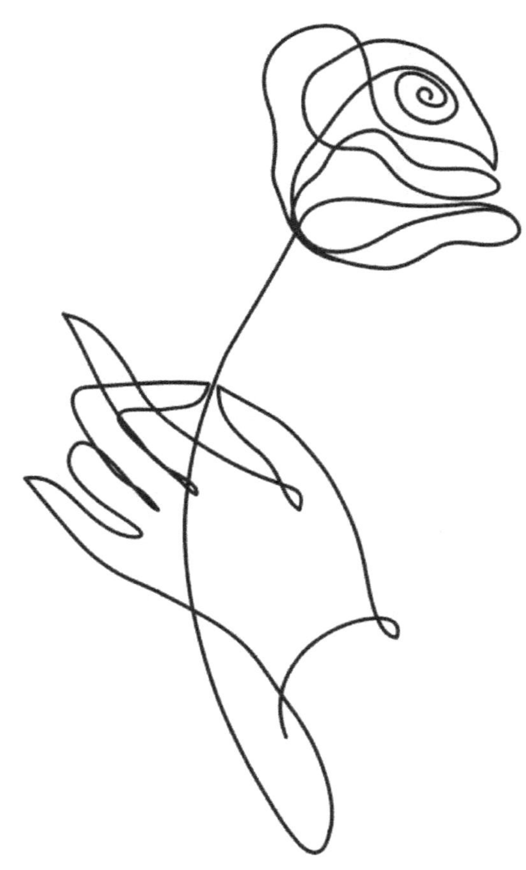

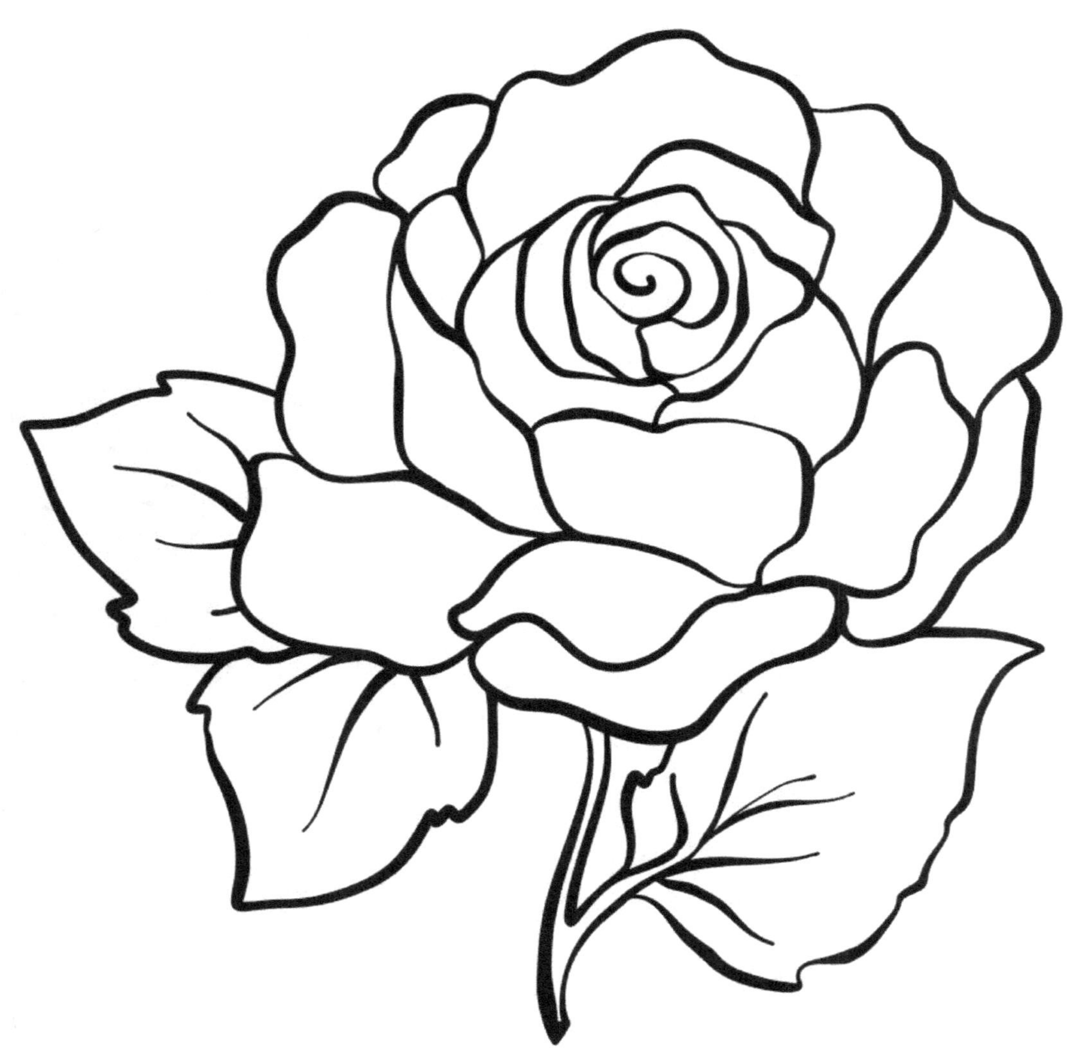

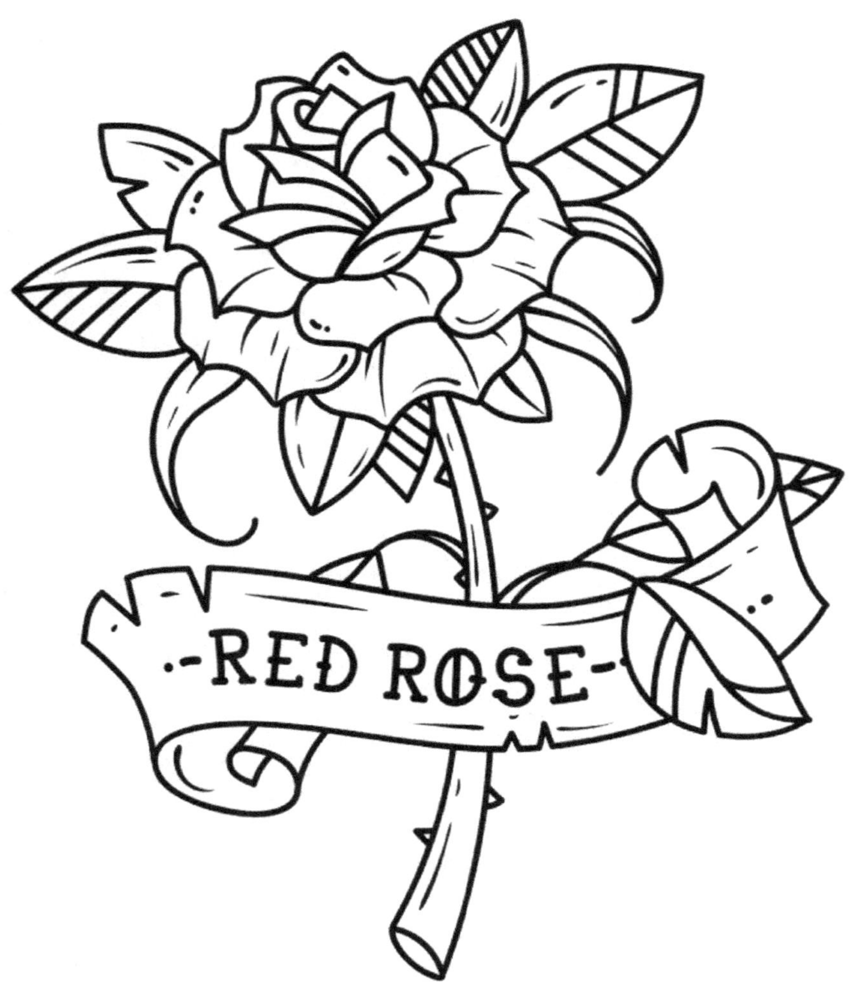

.-RED ROSE-.

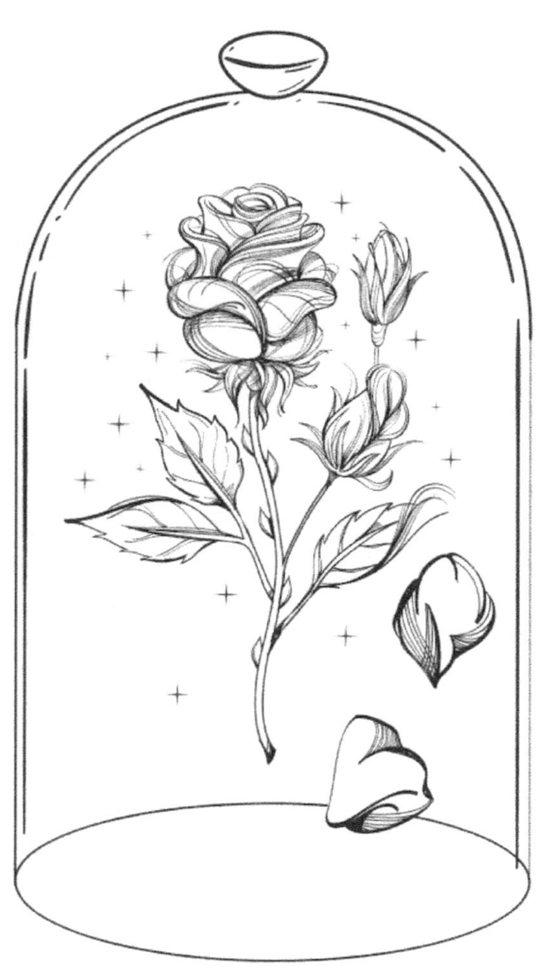

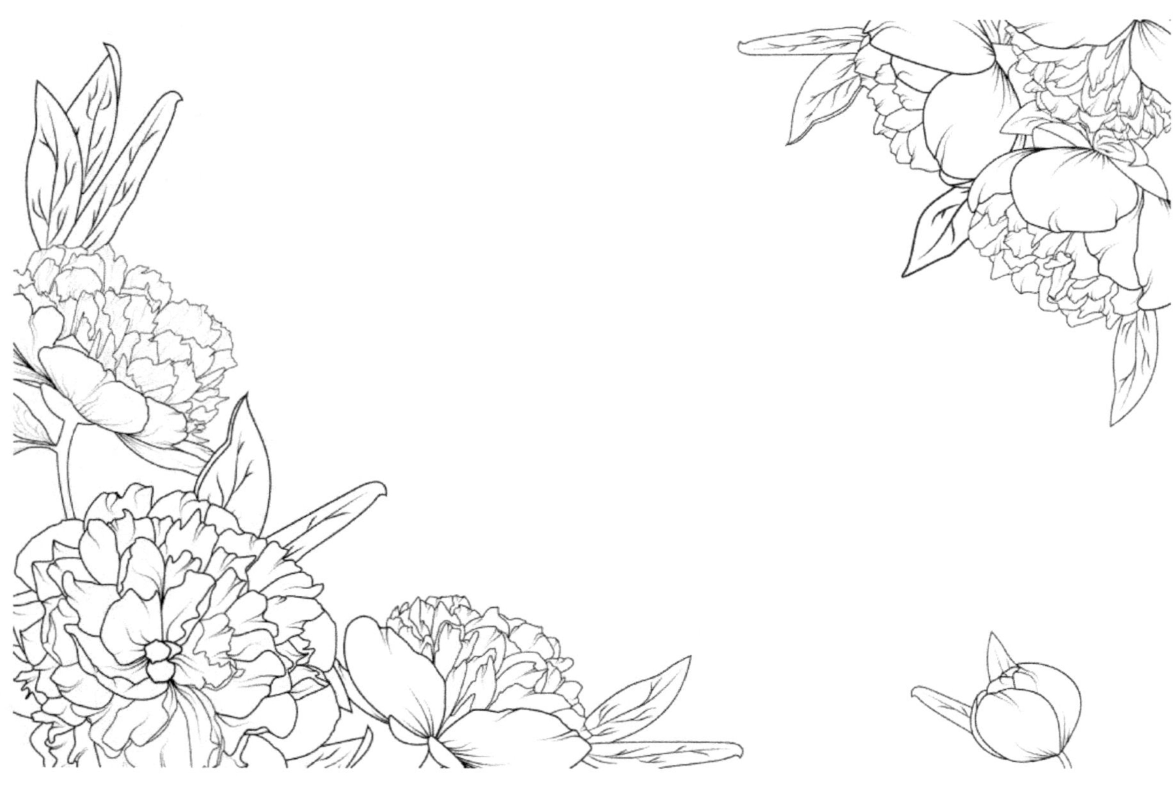

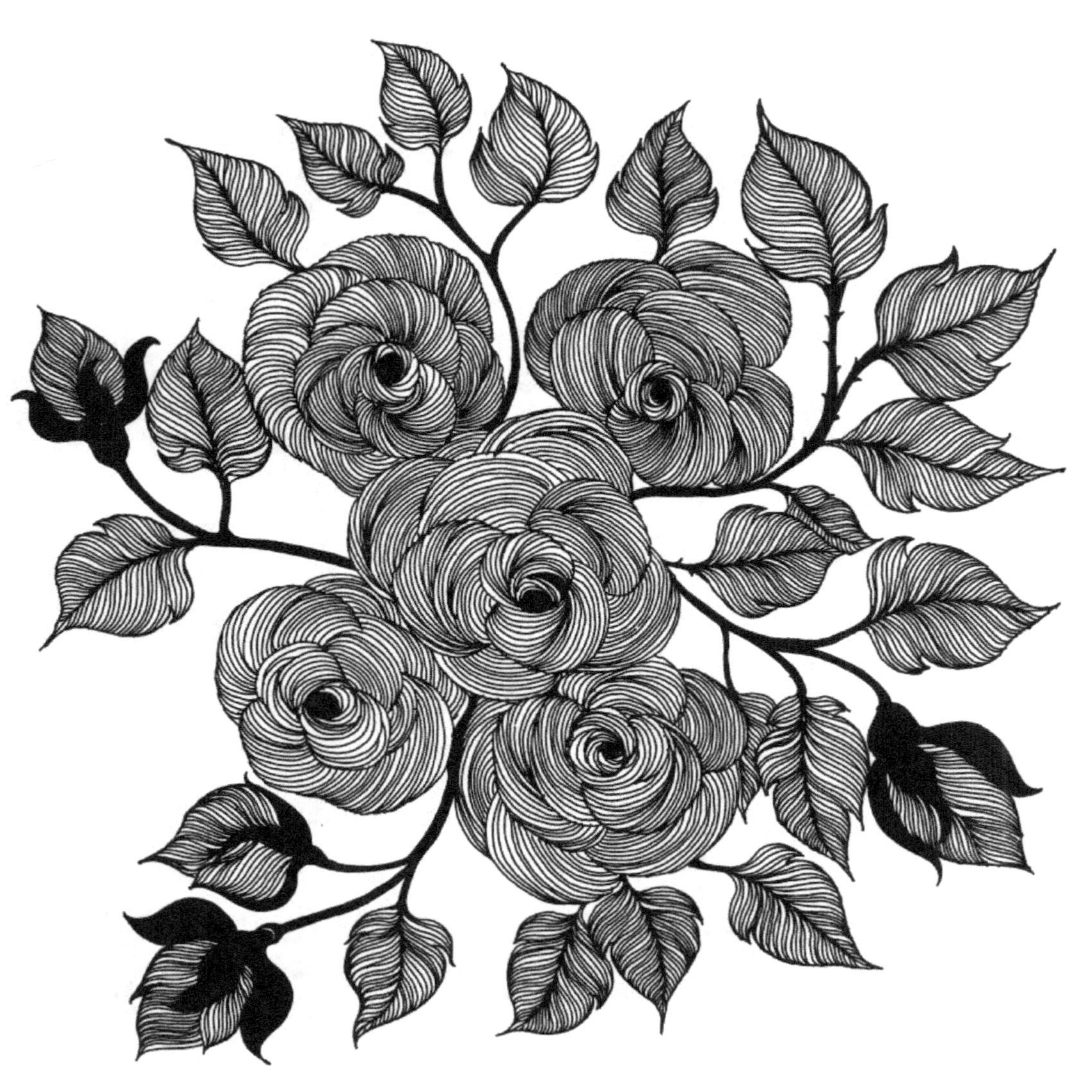

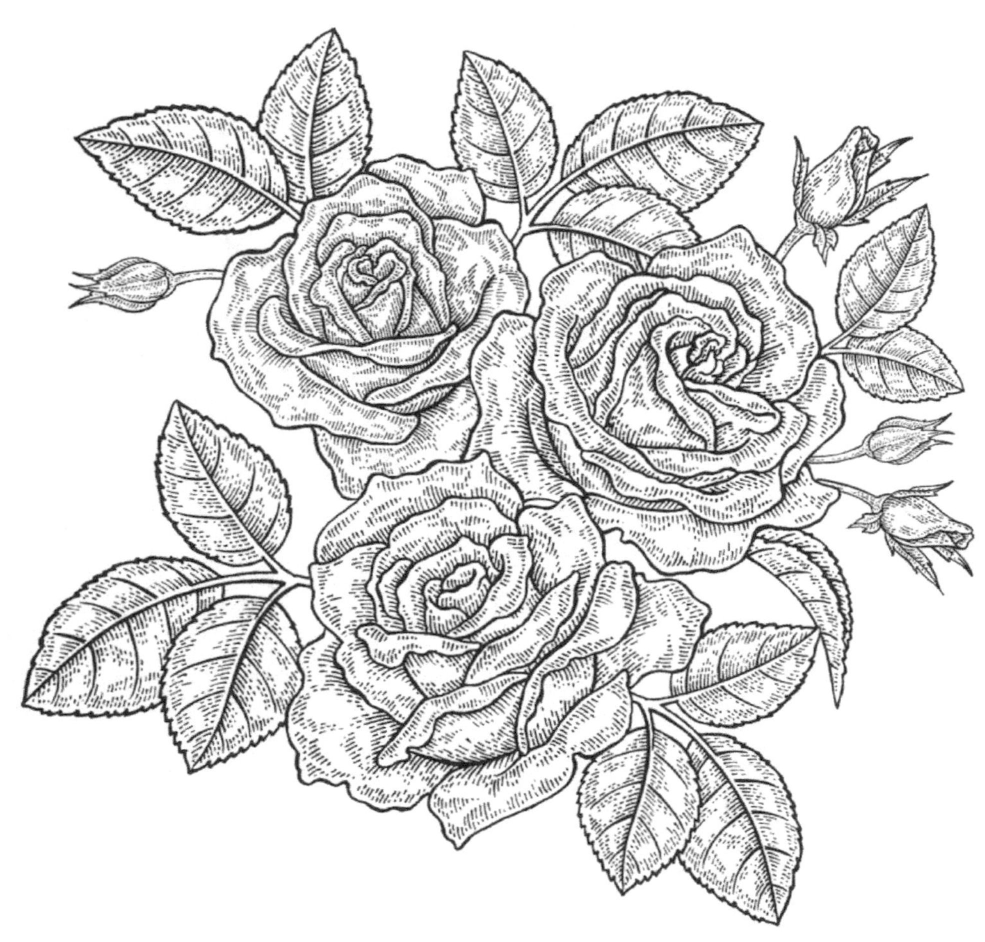

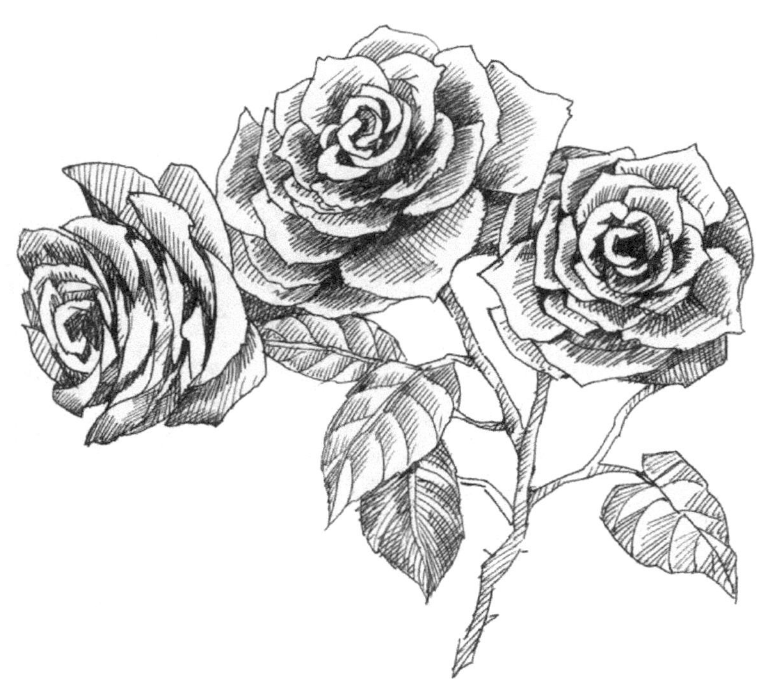

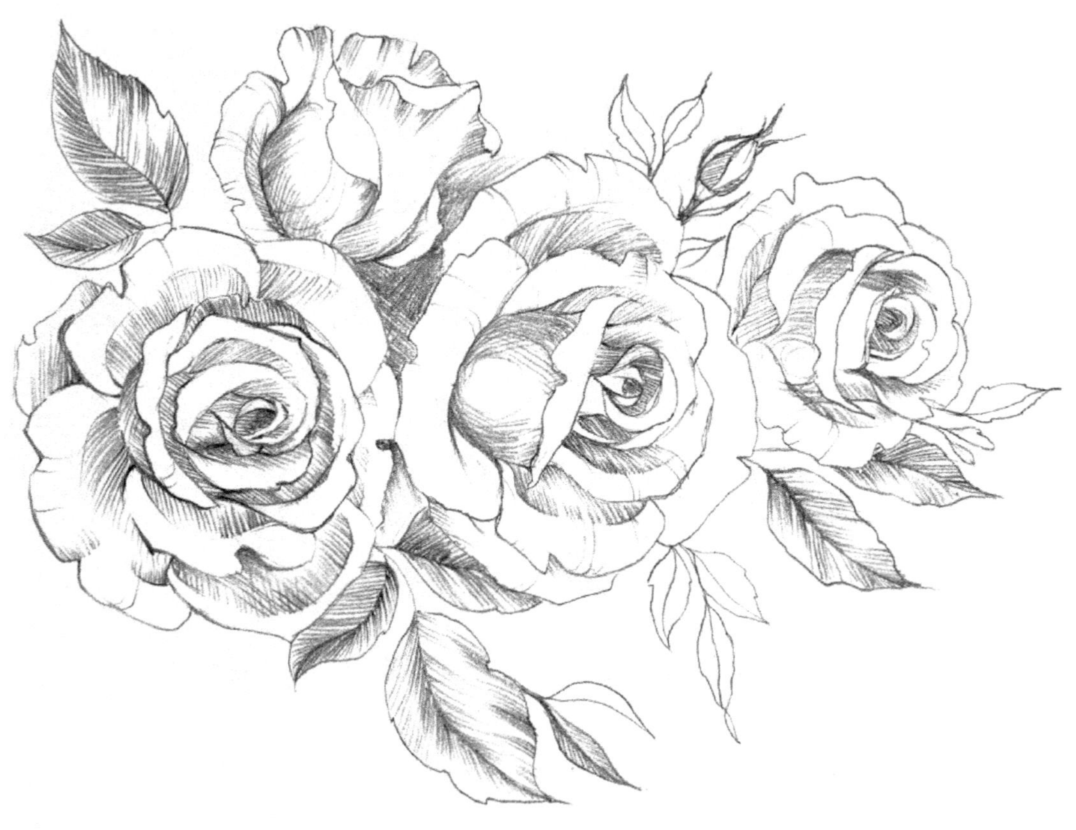

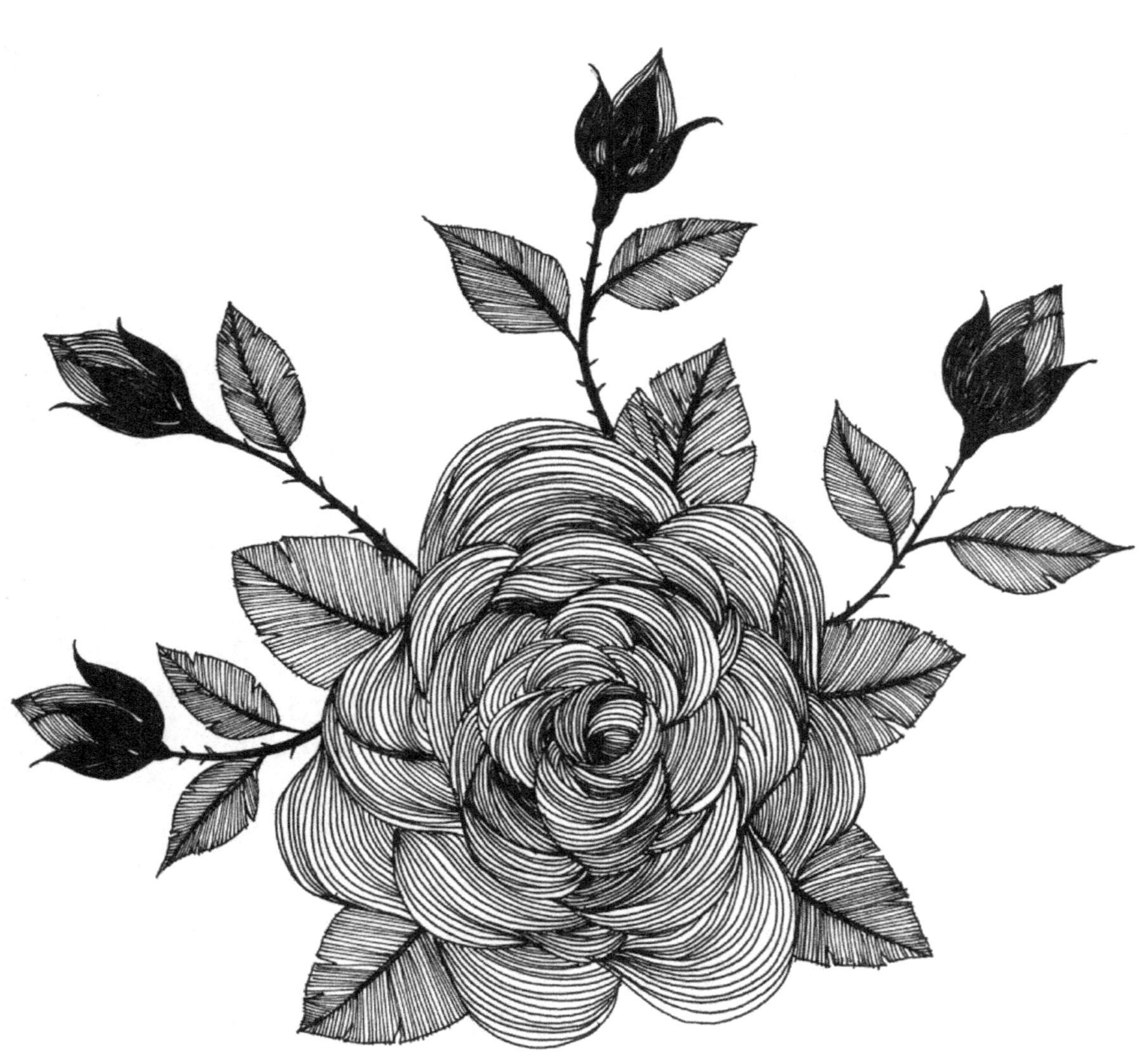

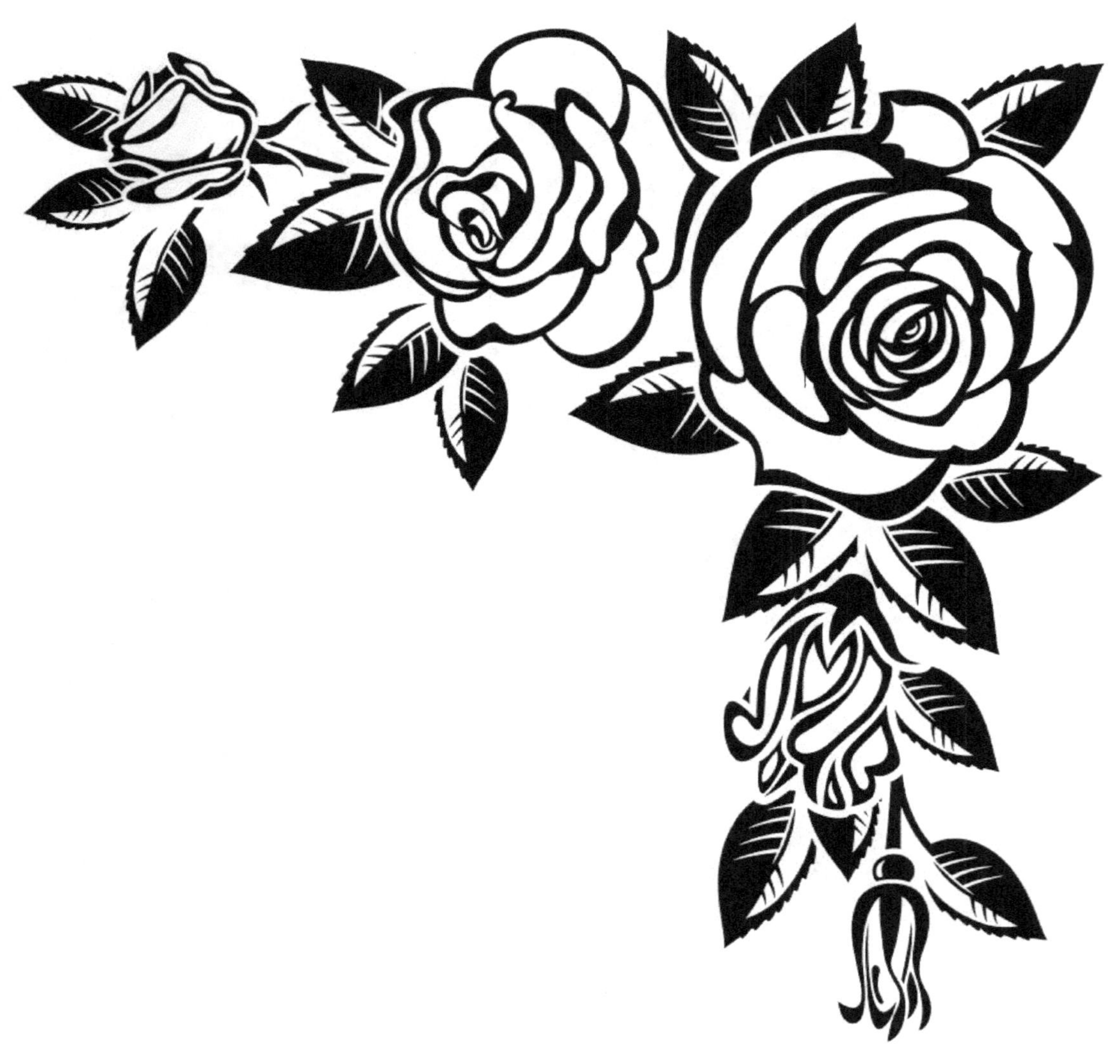

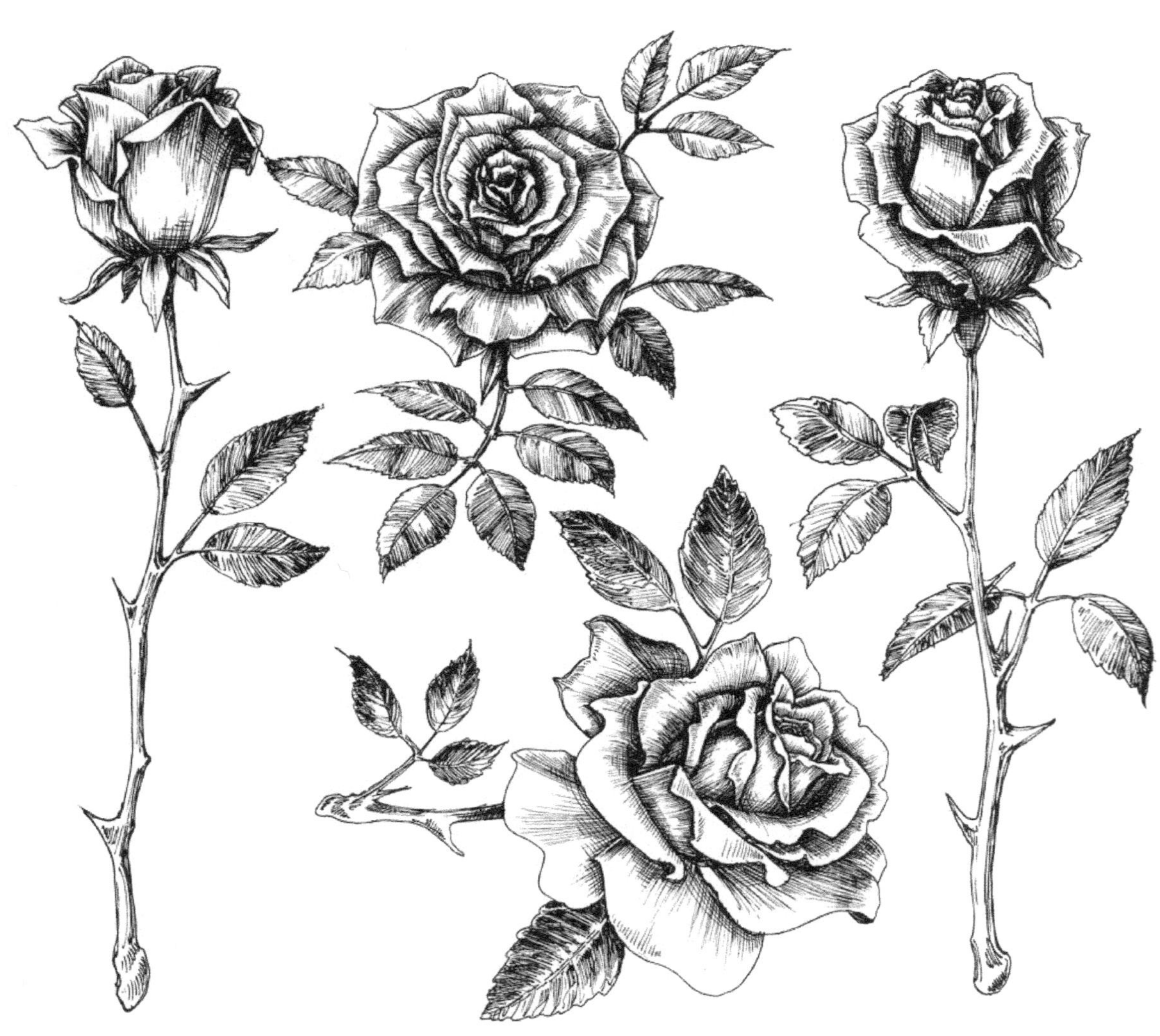

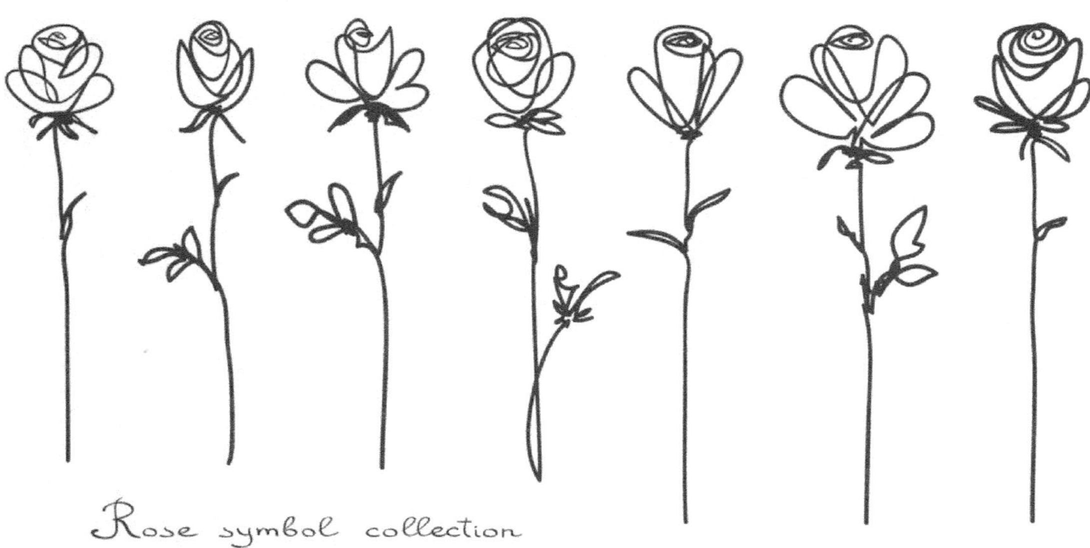
Rose symbol collection

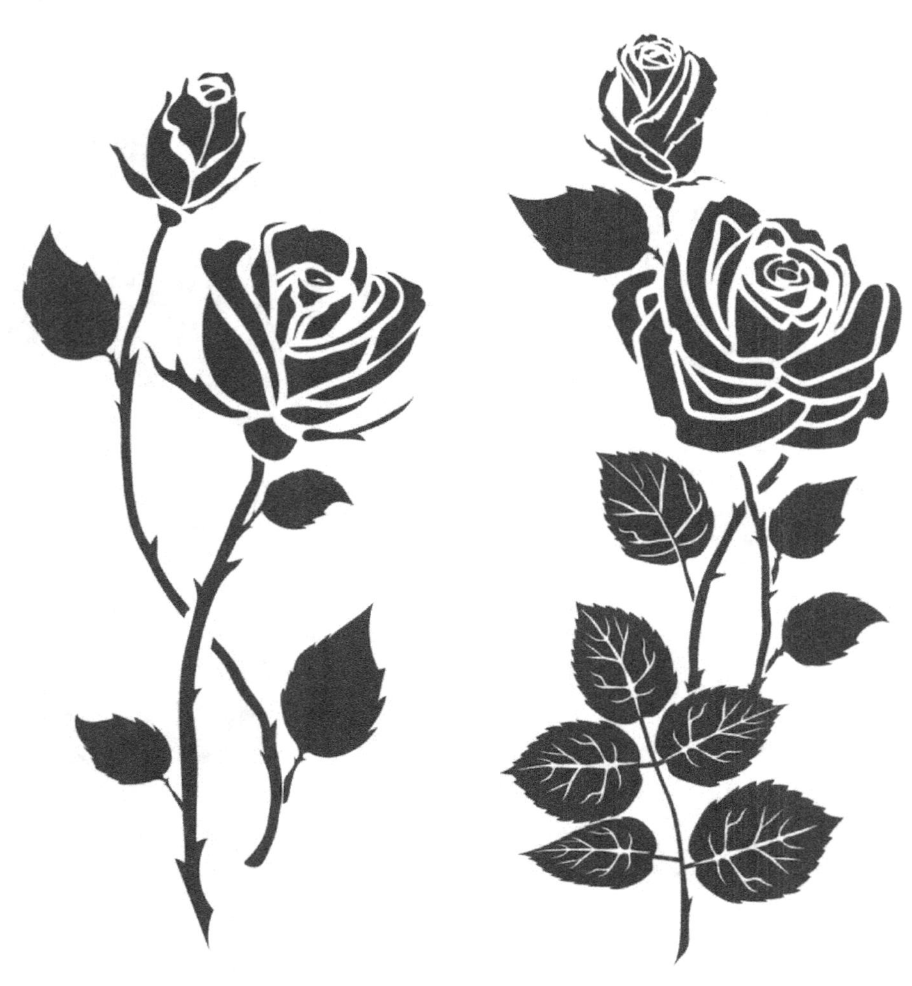

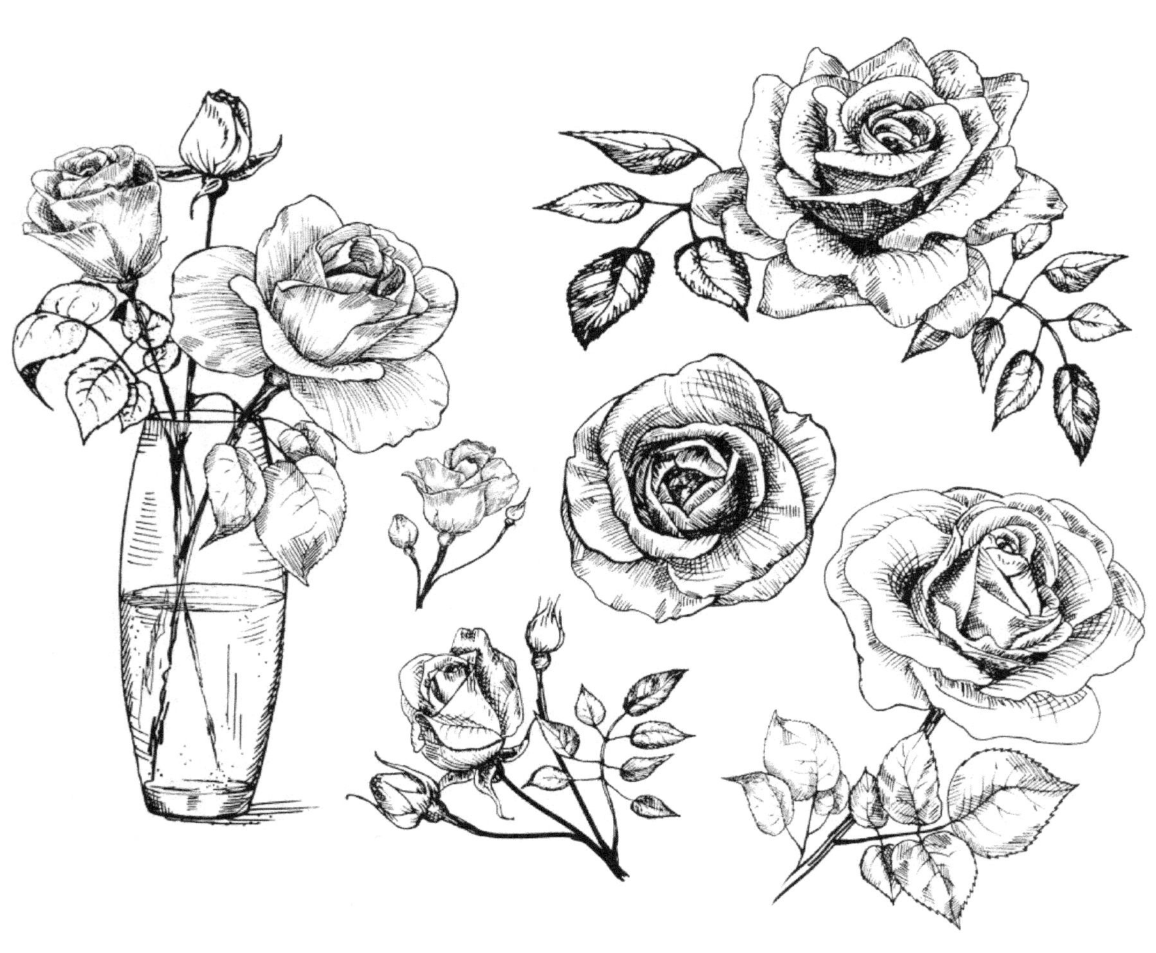

Beautiful roses
VECTOR

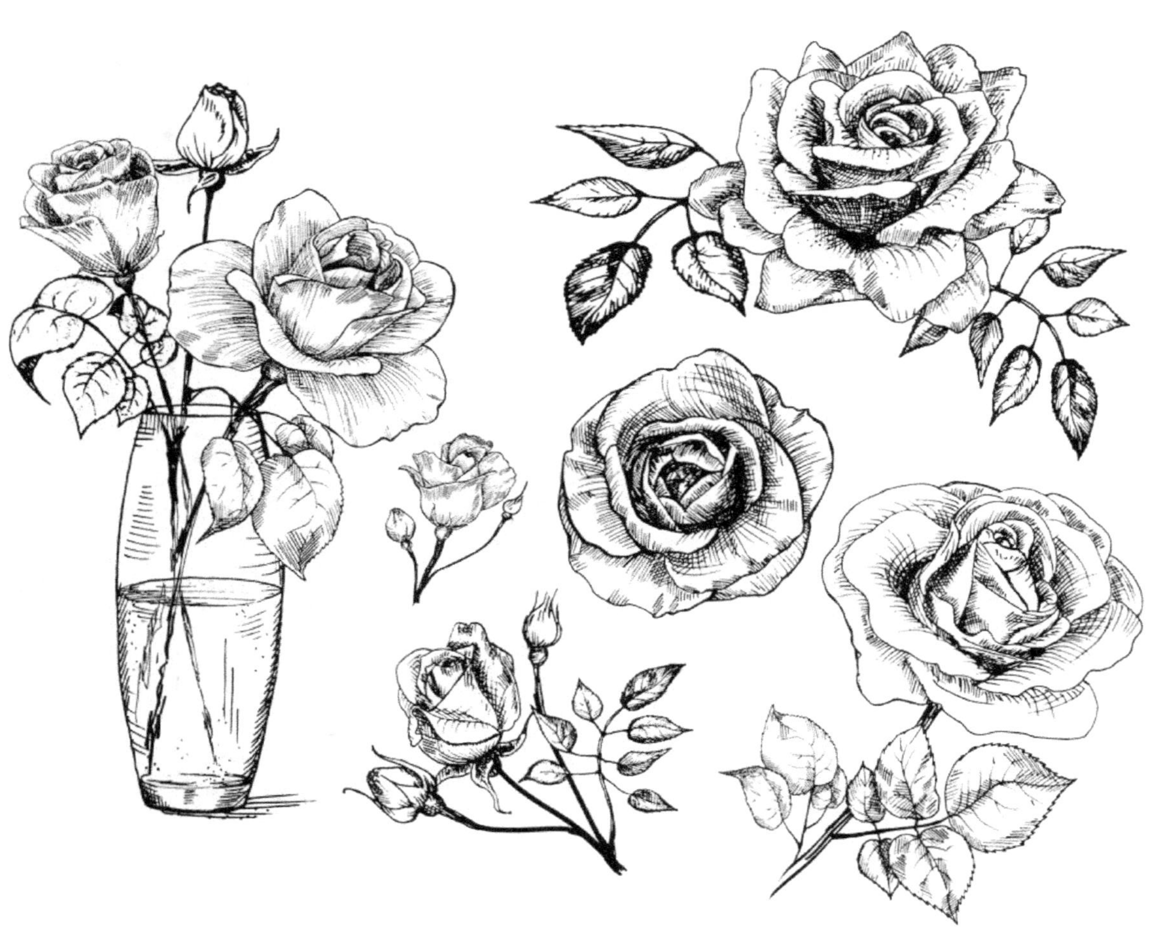

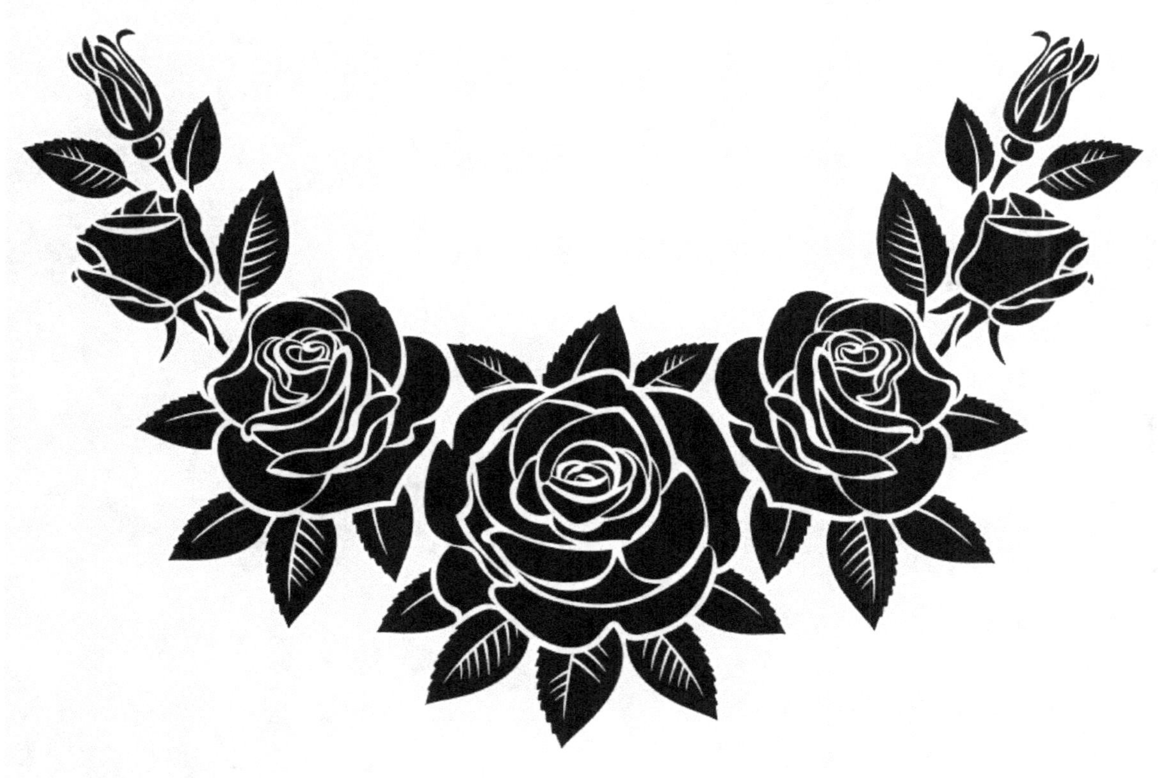

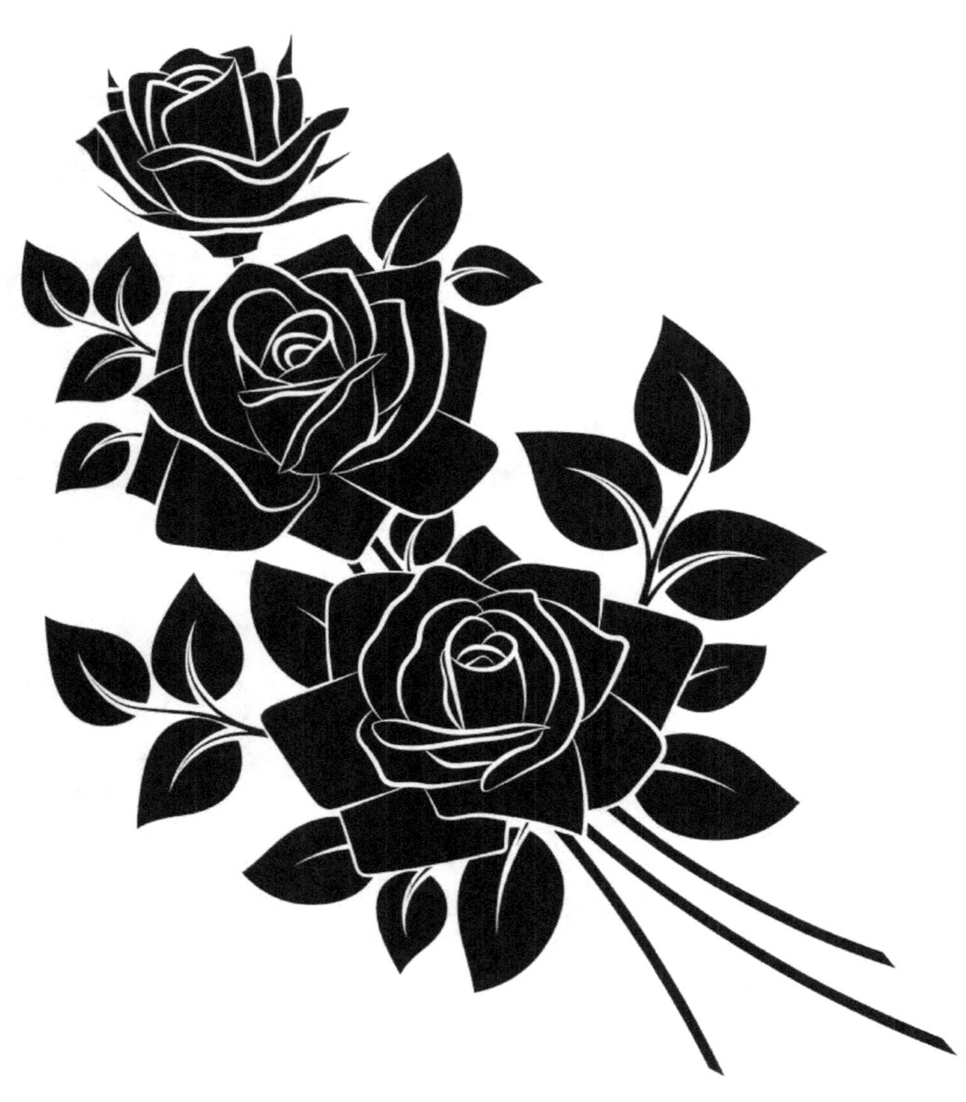

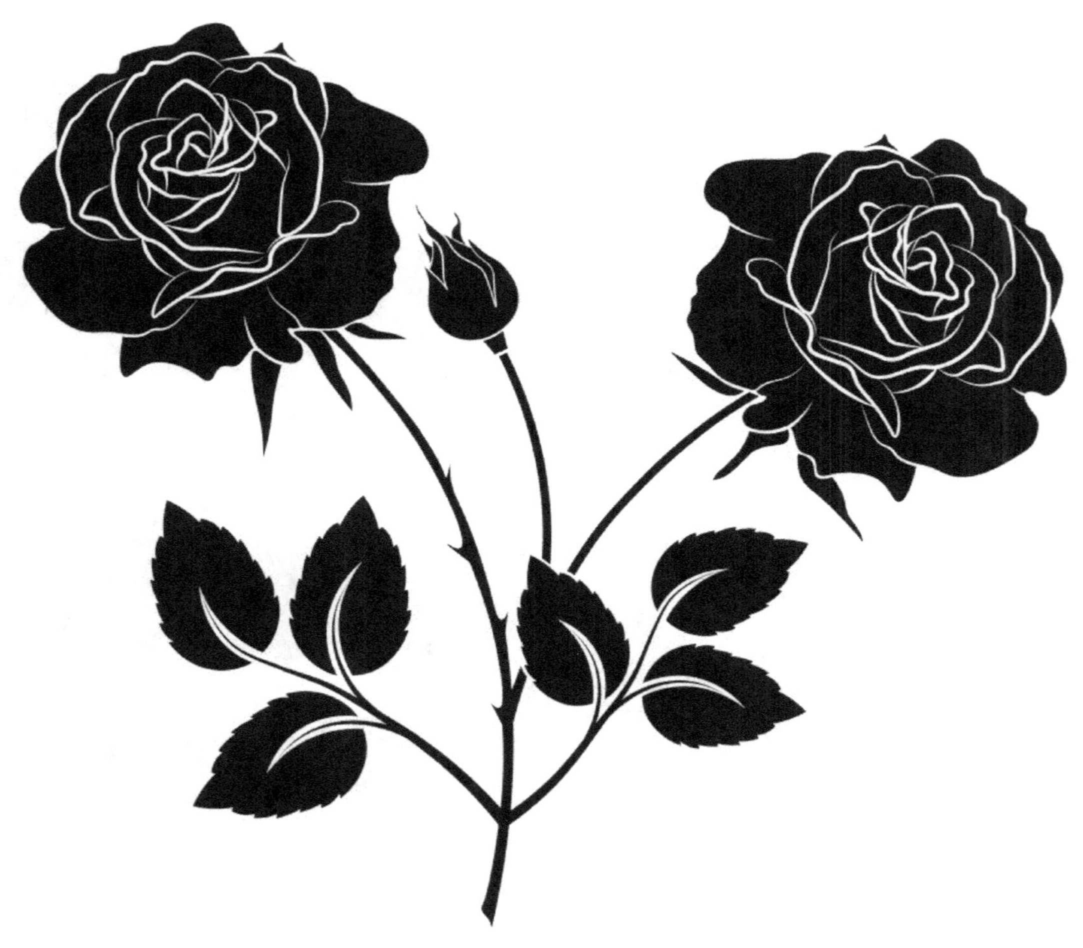

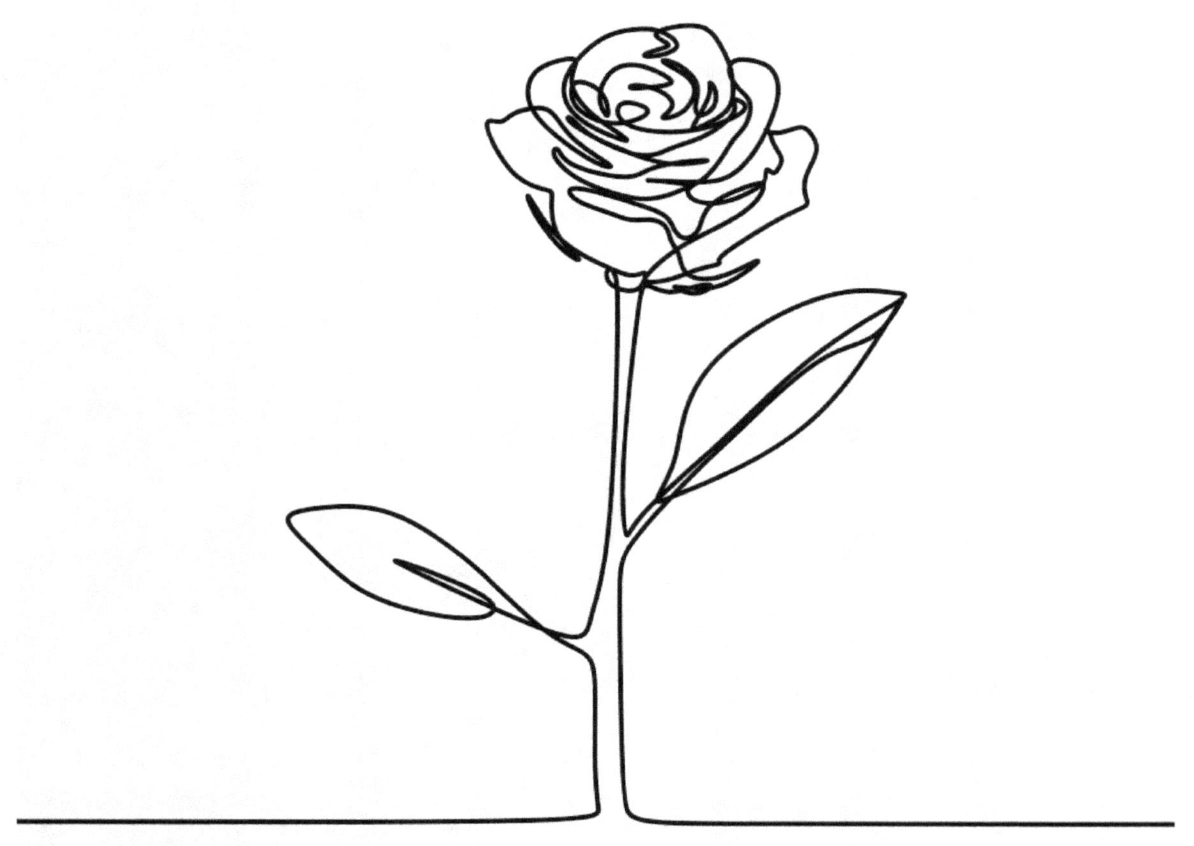

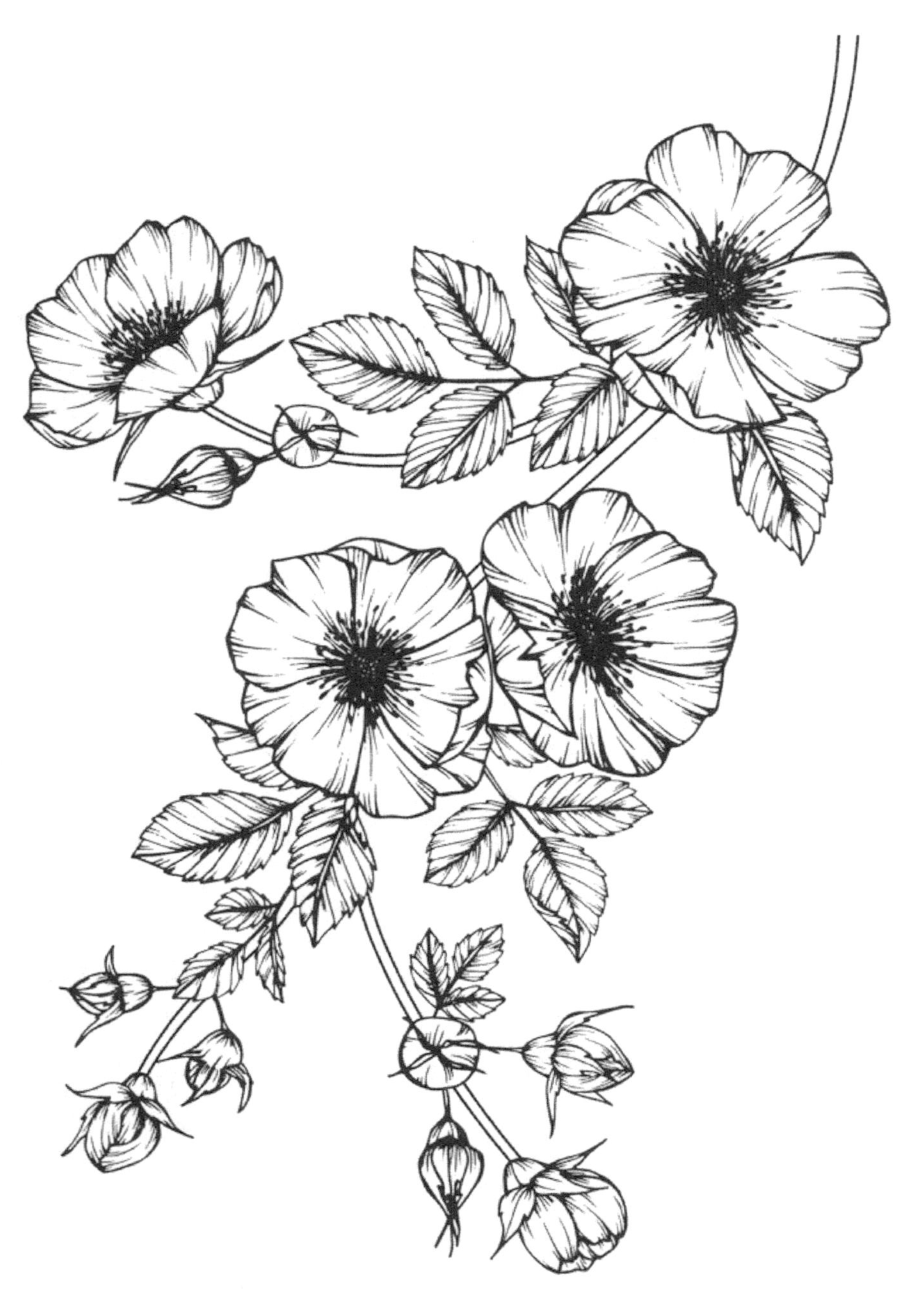

"WILD ROSE"

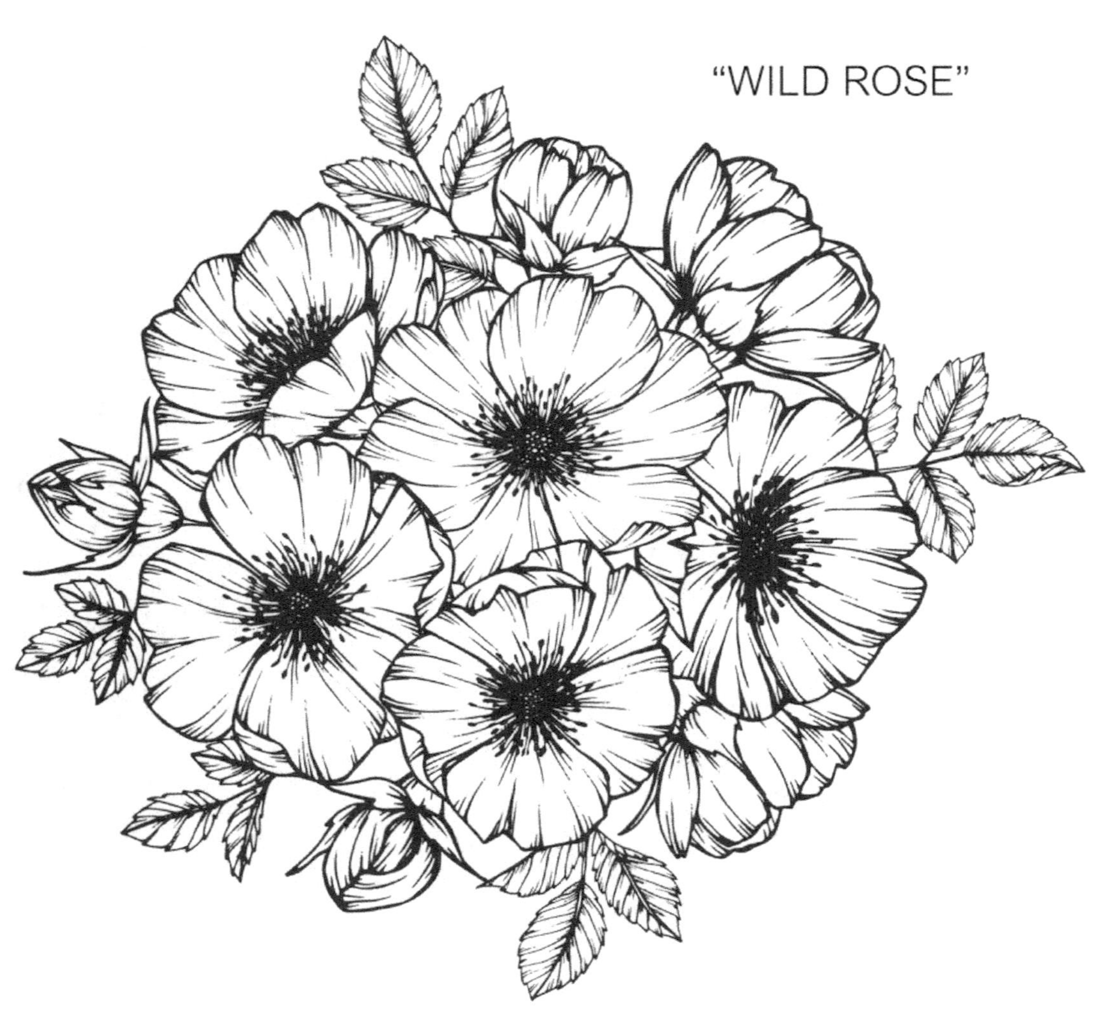

"WILD ROSE"

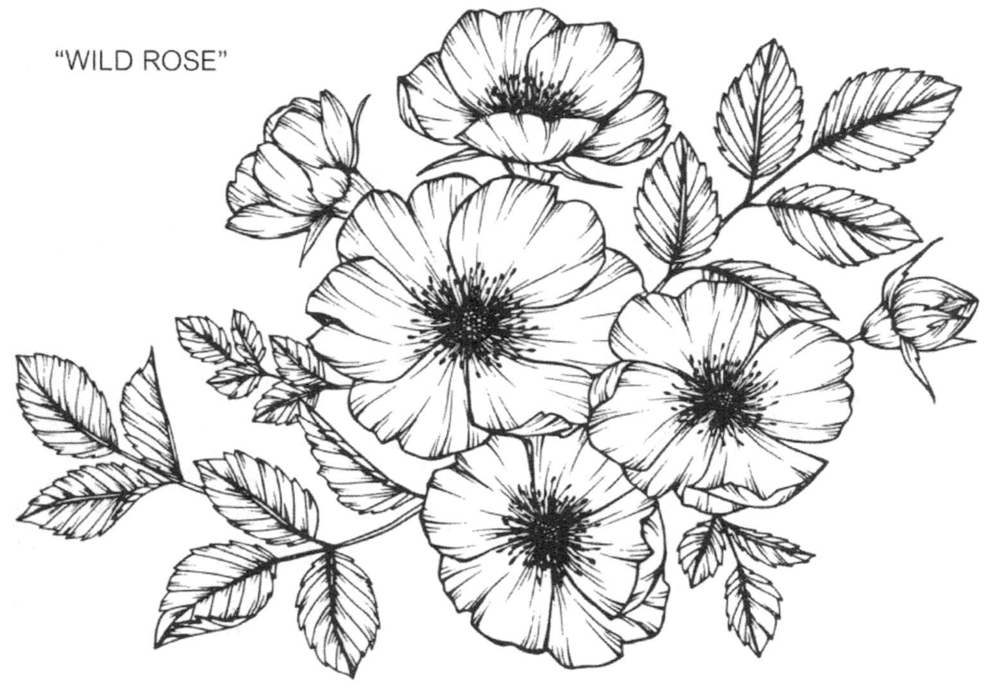

"WILD ROSE"